MINECRAFTER'S
COOKBOOK

THE MINECRAFTER'S COOKBOOK

MORE THAN 40

GAME-THEMED DINNERS, DESSERTS, SNACKS, AND DRINKS TO CRAFT TOGETHER

TARA THEOHARIS

SKY PONY PRESS
NEW YORK

Copyright © 2018 by Hollan Publishing, Inc.

Minecraft® is a registered trademark of Notch Development AB.

The Minecraft game is copyright © Mojang AB.

Sky Pony Press books may be purchased in bulk at special discounts for sales promotion, corporate gifts, fund-raising, or educational purposes. Special editions can also be created to specifications. For details, contact the Special Sales Department, Sky Pony Press, 307 West 36th Street, 11th Floor, New York, NY 10018 or info@skyhorsepublishing.com.

Sky Pony® is a registered trademark of Skyhorse Publishing, Inc.®, a Delaware corporation.

Minecraft® is a registered trademark of Notch Development AB. The Minecraft game is copyright © Mojang AB.

Visit our website at www.skyponypress.com.

10 9 8 7

Library of Congress Cataloging-in-Publication data is available on file.

Cover design by Brian Peterson
Interior design by Michael Short
Cover and interior art by Grace Sandford
Food styling by Jen Glovsky

Print ISBN: 978-1-5107-3969-7
EISBN: 978-1-5107-3970-3

Printed in China

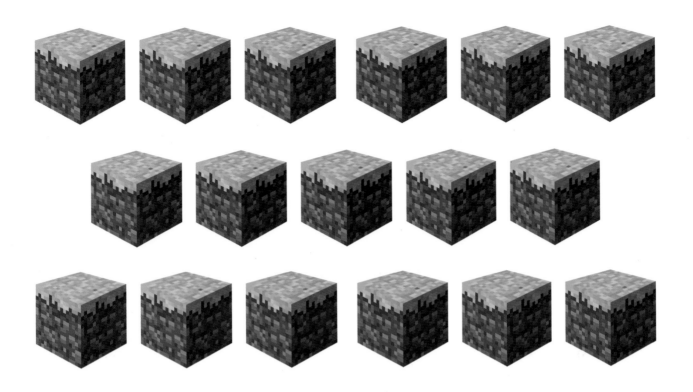

TO RHONDA MILLER, FOR INSTILLING A LOVE OF READING, COOKING,
AND CREATIVITY IN ME AT A YOUNG AGE.

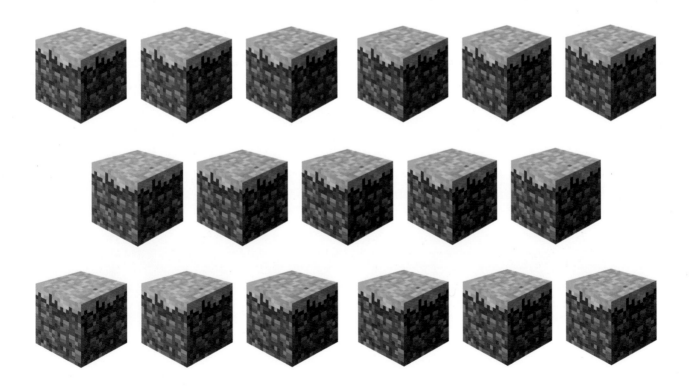

TABLE OF CONTENTS

INTRODUCTION

Welcome, Minecrafters! If you're reading this, you're on a mission to create something edible and epic, and this book is here to help.

In *Minecraft*, you can create whatever you want. In the kitchen, the same rules apply. But to create something truly amazing, you've got to practice, read tutorials, and level up. Just like you have favorite building materials (and maybe a few cheats) in the video game, you'll soon discover your favorite ingredients and tricks in the kitchen. And the more experience points you earn as a chef, the better you'll be at crafting delicious snacks, meals, desserts, and drinks.

The recipes in *The Minecrafter's Cookbook* allow you to create your favorite *Minecraft* foods and use real-life food to create some incredibly fun *Minecraft* items and characters from the game (think creepers, ghasts, diamonds, and chests)! Have a parent or adult help you read and follow the recipes, but be sure to get your hands messy and share what you know about the game as you go. You might even be inspired to create your own variations!

Ready to play? Here are some basics that will help you craft in the kitchen.

GATHER YOUR INVENTORY

You can't craft or brew without the necessary ingredients! Take a look at the recipe and make sure you have everything listed. All of these recipes are made with items you should be able to find at your local grocery store. If you can't find something, ask your grocer—they may be able to help you find a substitute!

STUDY THE RECIPE

Make sure you read the recipe all the way through before beginning. This will let you know if you need to prepare anything in advance, and how long the full recipe will take.

SET UP YOUR CRAFTING TABLE

When crafting, you need to have all of your items ready to go, and you must place them in the correct order. Cooking is exactly the same! Make sure all of your ingredients are prepared and easy to access before you start your recipe. This means that if something is meant to be chopped, peeled, or brought to room temperature, it's ready before you begin. Pay attention to the order of the recipe and follow it closely to be successful.

ASK FOR HELP

When you're not sure how to do something in *Minecraft*, you ask your friends or watch tutorials. Cooking is the same way! Not sure what something means, or how to create something the way you want? Ask your friends, a family member, or look online for a tutorial. It's the easiest way to gain xp! If you don't understand a word, check the glossary on page 107.

TRY OUT MODS

Just like in *Minecraft*, you can create your own mods for these recipes. Want to substitute one fruit for another? Prefer white chocolate to milk chocolate? Make these your own! Cooking is a science, so it's okay to experiment a little to make the dish that's tastiest to you. Think of cooking as being in creative mode. You've got all the blocks at your disposal, and the decisions are all yours.

Best of luck!

SNACKS

BAKED POTATOES

Makes: 1 serving

Baked potatoes will increase your health bar in and out of game. They're great for a snack or a meal, and are super simple to make. (You don't even need a furnace—just a real-life oven or microwave!) Once your potato is ready, have fun experimenting with a variety of toppings.

2

INGREDIENTS:

- 1 large potato
- 1 Tbsp. olive oil
- Salt
- Toppings (see sidebar)

TOOLS:

- Aluminum foil

DIRECTIONS:

1. Preheat oven to 350°F.
2. While preheating, wash the potato by scrubbing it with a brush under cold water.
3. Dry the potato and use a fork to poke holes all around the potato. (This will help moisture escape while it's cooking. Don't do this, and your potato might explode! Believe me. You do NOT want an exploded potato.)
4. Lightly coat the potato with olive oil. You can do this using a brush or your hands.
5. Sprinkle the potato with a pinch of salt and wrap it in aluminum foil.
6. Once the oven is preheated, place the foil-wrapped potato directly on the center oven rack.
7. Bake for 1 hour, then carefully remove the potato with pot holders.
8. Use a butter knife to cut the potato along the top, lengthwise.
9. Put the toppings of your choice on the potato and enjoy!

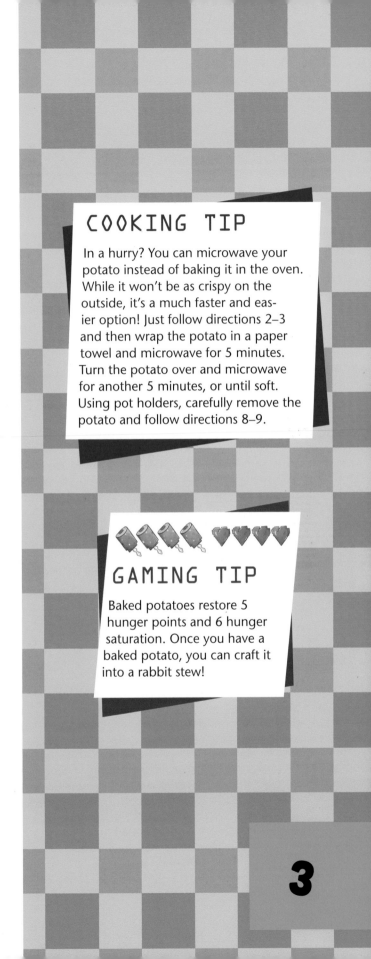

COOKING TIP

In a hurry? You can microwave your potato instead of baking it in the oven. While it won't be as crispy on the outside, it's a much faster and easier option! Just follow directions 2–3 and then wrap the potato in a paper towel and microwave for 5 minutes. Turn the potato over and microwave for another 5 minutes, or until soft. Using pot holders, carefully remove the potato and follow directions 8–9.

GAMING TIP

Baked potatoes restore 5 hunger points and 6 hunger saturation. Once you have a baked potato, you can craft it into a rabbit stew!

A baked potato can be topped with almost anything! You can keep it simple with some butter, salt, and pepper, or try some of the below (or anything else you can imagine!).

- Shredded cheese
- Crumbled bacon
- Sour cream
- Chives
- Chili
- Broccoli
- Black beans
- Salsa
- Mac and cheese
- Shredded chicken

CREATIVE MODE MUNCHIES

Makes: 4–6 servings

Creative mode is all about having fun building structures without the threat of zombies and creepers. Go into creative mode in your kitchen and play with your food! Use these fun snack foods, cut into cubes, to make structures just like the ones in-game.

INGREDIENTS:

- 3 oz. block of cheese
- Salami stick
- Melon (honeydew, cantaloupe, and watermelon all work!), quartered
- ½ French bread baguette, unsliced

TOOLS:
- Sharp knife
- Toothpicks

DIRECTIONS:

1. Cut the ingredients into cube shapes.
2. Play with your food! Stack the food any way you want and then snack away!

COOKING TIP

Building something epic? Use toothpicks to hold the different cubes together and create tall towers or beacons. Build a salami shelter and then use a cracker for the door to keep out hostile mobs. Just make sure you remove those toothpicks before eating your creation!

HAY BALE GRANOLA BARS

Makes: 8–12 servings (16 granola bars)

Hay is for horses, and these granola bars are full of things that horses (and humans) love! In-game, feed hay to horses, donkeys, and mules. In the kitchen, feed these granola bars (that only *look like* hay bales) to your whole family.

INGREDIENTS:

- 1 apple
- 2½ cups quick-cooking oats
- ½ cup sliced almonds
- 1 tsp. cinnamon
- 1 cup peanut butter
- ¼ cup honey

TOOLS:

- 8x8-inch square baking dish
- Wax paper
- Large bowl
- Small bowl
- Sharp knife

DIRECTIONS:

1. Line an 8x8-inch square baking dish with wax paper, letting the paper overlap over the sides. Set aside.
2. Peel and finely dice the apple.
3. Mix together the apple pieces, oats, almonds, and cinnamon into a large bowl.
4. In a small bowl, mix together the peanut butter and honey.
5. Pour the peanut butter/honey mixture over the contents of the large bowl. Mix until everything is combined.
6. Pour the contents of the bowl into the square pan. Using a sheet of wax paper, press down on the top, making sure it is packed in and the top is smooth and even.
7. Cover the dish and refrigerate for at least one hour.
8. Pull up on the wax paper to remove the granola from the dish.
9. Using a sharp knife, carefully cut into brick-shaped squares.
10. Keep the bars refrigerated for a few days, or individually wrapped and in a freezer bag in the freezer for longer storage.

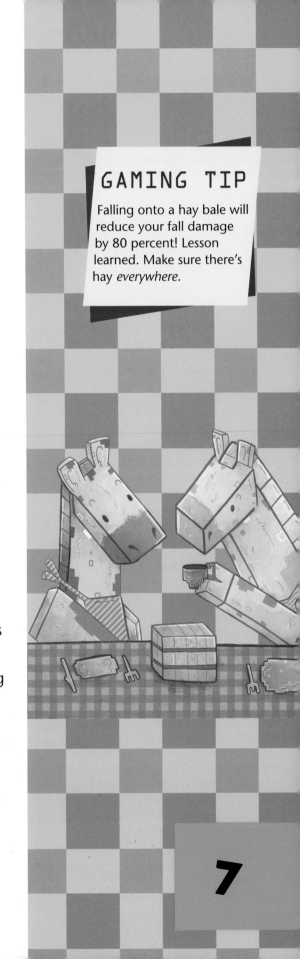

GAMING TIP

Falling onto a hay bale will reduce your fall damage by 80 percent! Lesson learned. Make sure there's hay *everywhere*.

CHORUS FRUIT SALAD

Makes: 4–6 servings

I wish chorus fruit existed in real life. A delicious fruit that might also teleport you? It would make life so much more fun! The closest things to chorus fruit in real life are blueberries, and while they won't teleport you, they ARE delicious. We're mixing them in with a "chorus" of other fruits and a honey-citrus dressing to make a fruit salad you'll want to gobble up!

8

INGREDIENTS:

- 1 pint blueberries
- 1 pint strawberries
- 1 bunch red grapes
- 3 kiwis
- 2 bananas
- ¼ cup honey
- Juice of a fresh squeezed lemon or lime (around 2 Tbsp.)

TOOLS:

- Sharp knife
- Large bowl
- Peeler
- Small bowl

DIRECTIONS:

1. Rinse and pat dry the blueberries, strawberries, and grapes.
2. Cut the top off of the strawberries, and then quarter them.
3. Place the blueberries, grapes, and quartered strawberries into a large bowl.
4. Peel the skin from the kiwis, and then cut into slices. Cut the slices in half and add the kiwi to the bowl.
5. Peel the bananas and slice. Add to the bowl.
6. In a small bowl, stir the honey with the fresh-squeezed lime or lemon juice.
7. Pour the juice mixture over the fruit and mix together.

COOKING TIP

Have a favorite fruit that's not in this salad? Are some of these fruits not in season? Substitute them. Experiment by mixing a combination of your favorite fruits together.

GAMING TIP

Chorus fruit will restore 4 hunger points and 2.4 hunger saturation, but be careful: there's a chance you'll be teleported when you eat it!

FARMER'S DELIGHT PUMPKIN SEEDS

Makes: 4–6 servings

Pumpkin seeds help you fill your hunger bar in the game of *Minecraft*—they also make a delicious snack in real life! Next fall, hang onto the seeds you scoop out when you're carving pumpkins, and turn them into this crunchy, salty treat.

10

INGREDIENTS:

- 1 pumpkin's worth of seeds
- 3 cups water
- 3 Tbsp. salt

TOOLS:

- Strainer
- Large bowl
- Baking sheet
- Spatula

DIRECTIONS:

1. Place your seeds into a strainer and rinse until they're completely clean.
2. Fill a large bowl with 3 cups of water and 3 Tbsp. salt. Mix together to make salt water. Place the seeds in the bowl and let sit for 15 minutes. While the pumpkins are sitting, preheat your oven to 150°F (or as low as it can go).
3. Drain the pumpkin seeds in the strainer, but do not rinse.
4. Spread the seeds out onto a baking sheet, and then place in the oven.
5. Keep in the oven for 4 hours, or until they are fully dried out, turning them over with a spatula once every hour. At the midway point, spritz with some water and sprinkle more salt on them.
6. Once they are fully dry, change the oven temperature to 250°F and roast for 10 minutes.

GAMING TIP

Need to break a pumpkin fast? Grab an axe! Axes break pumpkins the fastest in survival mode.

GAMING TIP

Pumpkins aren't just for eating in the game of *Minecraft*. Wearing a pumpkin on your head actually keeps Enderman from attacking. You can also use pumpkins to craft helpful mobs called iron golems!

GOLDEN CARROT DIP

Makes: 10 servings (2 Tbsp. each)

This dip will turn any carrot golden, and make it taste even better in the process! But don't limit yourself to just carrots: use it for veggies or chicken, or turn it into a dressing and drizzle it over a salad!

INGREDIENTS:

- ¾ cup plain Greek yogurt
- ¼ cup mustard
- ¼ cup honey
- Salt and pepper (optional)

TOOLS:

- Whisk
- Small bowl

COOKING TIP

Want to turn this dip into a dressing or marinade? Whisk in 1 Tbsp. of white vinegar.

GAMING TIP

Use golden carrots to get cute, little rabbits to follow you around in the game.

DIRECTIONS:

1. Whisk together the yogurt, mustard, and honey in a bowl.
2. Season with salt and pepper.
3. Serve as a dip for carrots and cut veggies.

MINI GLISTERING MELONS

Makes: 10 servings, (40 mini melons)

These miniature glistering melons aren't melons at all! Instead, they're a fun sweet treat encased in a lime rind for you and your friends. Make them glisten with the addition of shimmering sprinkles. This recipe makes plenty of treats and they are a huge hit at parties.

INGREDIENTS:

- 10 limes
- 1 box (3 oz.) watermelon-flavored gelatin (or any red-colored gelatin)
- 1 cup water, boiling
- 1 cup water, cold
- Gold shimmering sprinkles

TOOLS:

- Sharp knife
- Rimmed baking sheet or casserole dish

DIRECTIONS:

1. Cut the limes in half lengthwise and juice the limes. (We won't need the lime juice for this recipe. You can use it to make the Chorus Fruit Salad on page 8.)
2. Carefully remove the pulp from the lime rinds. We want to make the rinds as smooth as possible!
3. Place the empty lime rind cups into a rimmed baking sheet or casserole dish so they're all sitting up and touching each other, ready to be filled.
4. Mix the gelatin and the boiling water until it has completely dissolved.
5. Add the cold water and mix.
6. Carefully pour the gelatin mixture into the lime cups, filling them nearly to the top.
7. Refrigerate the cups for 2–4 hours or until fully set.
8. Carefully cut each cup in half, forming melon-shaped wedges.
9. Sprinkle the wedges with gold sprinkles.

COOKING TIP

Still have some leftover lime juice? Make limeade! Just mix 1 cup lime juice, 1 cup sugar, and 5 cups water in a pitcher until the sugar is dissolved.

GAMING TIP

You can make a glistering melon in the game by combining 8 gold nuggets and a melon. You can't eat it, but you can use it to brew a mundane potion or a potion of healing.

ICE BLOCKS

Makes: 3–4 servings (12 ice blocks)

Brr! You don't have to go to a snowy biome to find these ice blocks. These cold and healthy snacks look just like *Minecraft* ice blocks, but taste much better. If you want a smoother, more uniform look, blend the berries and yogurt together before adding to the molds.

INGREDIENTS:

- 1½ cups vanilla or blueberry yogurt
- 1 cup blueberries

TOOLS:

- Medium bowl
- Ice cube mold

GAMING TIP

When you think of sure-footed animals, you rarely think of pigs. But here's a fun fact: If you throw a saddle on a pig and ride it over icy plains, you'll travel much faster than you would on foot.

DIRECTIONS:

1. Mix the yogurt and the blueberries in a bowl.
2. Spoon the yogurt mixture into square ice cube molds.
3. Freeze for 2+ hours.
4. Once frozen, remove from the ice molds. These will last 1–2 months in the freezer.

COOKING TIP

Make multiple types of ice blocks in a variety of colors! Use lime yogurt to make slime blocks. Blend vanilla yogurt with strawberries to make pink blocks, blackberries to make purple blocks, and mango for orange blocks. Want pure white blocks? Don't bother with the berries; just freeze some vanilla yogurt!

NOT-SO-ROTTEN FLESH

Makes: 4 servings

Let's face it, if rotten flesh had been soaked in a marinade and dried in an oven for a few hours, it probably wouldn't be so rotten. What a waste. Lucky for you, this dried "not-so-rotten flesh" will fill your hunger bar without any risk of food poisoning.

INGREDIENTS:

- 1 lb. flank steak (as lean as you can get it)
- ⅔ cups soy sauce
- ⅔ cups Worcestershire sauce
- 2 Tbsp. brown sugar
- 1 tsp. paprika
- 1 tsp. garlic powder
- 1 tsp. onion powder
- 1 tsp. black pepper
- ½ tsp. salt

TOOLS:

- Large, sharp knife
- Large freezer bag
- Large bowl
- Two baking sheets
- Aluminum foil
- Two wire racks
- Paper towels
- Airtight container

DIRECTIONS:

1. To cut your steak into strips, freeze it for an hour and then have an adult with a large, sharp knife cut it into as thin of strips as you can manage, less than ¼-inch thick. Cut with the grain if you want traditional chewy jerky, or against the grain if you want the jerky to be a bit more tender and brittle. Cut off any large pieces of fat you see on the slices.
2. Place the steak slices into a large, zippered freezer bag.
3. Mix the rest of the ingredients in a bowl until the sugar has dissolved.
4. Pour the contents of the bowl into the bag, seal, and move around the steak so it's fully covered.
5. Let the steak marinate in the refrigerator overnight (or at least 3 hours).
6. Preheat the oven to 175°F (or as low as your oven will go) and cover two baking sheets with aluminum foil. Place a wire rack over each baking sheet.
7. Remove the steak from the marinade and gently pat with a paper towel to remove extra marinade.
8. Lay the steak out on the wire racks and place into the oven.
9. Cook for 4 hours.
10. Check on the meat. Is it dry and leathery? It should crack when you bend it, but not completely break. If it's not dry enough for you, place back in the oven and continue to check every 30 minutes. (The time it takes to fully dry will depend on the thickness of your meat, temperature of your oven, and your personal preferences.)
11. Let cool. Store in an airtight container in the refrigerator for up to one month.

PRETZEL STICK TORCHES

Makes: 3–4 servings (12 torches)

You won't survive a night in *Minecraft* without some torches. They keep away the bad guys and help you find your way home. Let these fun pretzel torches light the way to an exciting snacktime adventure!

INGREDIENTS:

- 1 cup white chocolate chips
- 12 pretzel sticks
- Red and yellow sparkling sprinkles

TOOLS:

- Baking sheet
- Wax paper
- Microwave-safe bowl
- Small bowls

DIRECTIONS:

1. Prep a baking sheet or other smooth surface with wax paper.
2. Place the white chocolate chips in a microwave-safe bowl, and heat in a microwave for 30 seconds. Stir. Continue heating in 30-second intervals and stirring until the chocolate is melted and smooth.
3. Dip the end of each pretzel stick into the melted white chocolate.
4. Dip the white chocolate end into the red and yellow sparkling sugar.
5. Place the sticks onto the wax paper until chocolate is cooled and hardened.

COOKING TIP

Want to dress up the torches a bit? Use red or yellow candy melts instead of white chocolate chips!

GAMING TIP

Exploring somewhere dark? Place torches only on the right side. That way if you can get lost, you can check the torches. If the torches are still on your right, you're on your way in. If they're on the left, you must be on your way out!

SPAWN EGGS

Makes: 4–6 servings (6 eggs)

You may think eggs can only be used as ingredients for baked goods and throwables in *Minecraft*, but certain eggs can spawn mobs! These spawn eggs are brightly colored, and each egg represents a different mob, like a zombie, a ghast, or a blaze. We'll make our own version by hard-boiling and dying some monstrously fun eggs.

INGREDIENTS:

- 6 eggs
- Food coloring in the colors of your choice
- 1 Tbsp. white vinegar (per color)
- Salt and pepper (optional)

TOOLS:

- Pot with a lid
- Tall glasses
- Crayons

DIRECTIONS:

1. Carefully place the eggs into a pot, so they all lay flat along the bottom.
2. Fill the pot with cold water until it's at least an inch above the eggs.
3. Place the pot on the stove and turn the temperature to "high" until the water begins to boil.
4. As soon as the water boils, cover the pot and remove it from heat.
5. Let sit for 15 minutes. (The eggs will keep cooking in the hot water!)
6. While the eggs are cooking, prepare the food coloring by filling a tall glass with 5–10 drops of food coloring, 1 Tbsp. vinegar, and water until it's halfway full. Create one of these for each color.
7. Rinse the eggs with cold water. Use a crayon to add spots if desired.
8. Add a couple of eggs to each glass of food coloring, and let sit in the fridge for at least 4 hours. The longer you leave it in, the darker the color will be.
9. Use your crayons to add designs and decorations to your spawn eggs.
10. When ready to eat, carefully peel the egg and enjoy with a dash of salt and pepper.

There are 43 different spawn eggs available in all editions of *Minecraft*. How many can you design? Use this chart for inspiration.

SPAWN EGG	COLOR
• Ghast	• white with gray spots
• Zombie	• blue with green spots
• Wolf	• white with brown spots
• Blaze	• yellow
• Pig	• pink
• Slime	• green

VILLAGE FARMER'S BREAD

Makes: 1 loaf of bread

Yes, bread does involve a lot of wheat, as shown in-game. But there's more to it in real life than 3 wheats and a crafting table. Learn to make your own loaf of bread with this simple recipe that uses flour, yeast, and salt. Once you've made a basic loaf, get creative and try the flavor combinations listed here.

22

INGREDIENTS:

- 3 cups flour (plus more for dusting)
- ½ tsp. instant yeast
- 2 tsp. salt
- 1½ cups lukewarm water

TOOLS:

- Large bowl
- Plastic wrap
- Dutch oven or oven-safe pot
- Parchment paper
- Wire cooling rack

COOKING TIP

Want to make your bread a bit more fun? Try some of these flavor combinations by mixing in the listed ingredients during step #1!

- 2 Tbsp. rosemary, and then top the bread with sea salt once you put it into your pot.
- ½ cup shredded cheese (Asiago or cheddar are delicious, but your favorite cheese will do!)
- A head of garlic (slice the cloves in half lengthwise) and ¼ cup parmesan cheese
- ¾ cup raisins, and sprinkle your work surface with cinnamon sugar when forming the dough into a ball. Sprinkle a bit more on top once it's in the pot.
- ¼ cup cocoa powder, ¼ cup sugar, and 1 cup chocolate chips for a chocolate bread!

DIRECTIONS:

1. In a large bowl, combine flour, yeast, and salt. Add water to the mixture and stir until blended and sticky.
2. Cover the bowl with plastic wrap and let rest at room temperature for 12 hours. The dough will bubble up and rise.
3. Place a Dutch oven or other large oven-safe pot with a lid in the oven, and preheat the oven to 450°F. Keep the pot in the oven for 30 minutes.
4. While the oven and pot are heating, sprinkle flour over a cutting board or other work surface and put the dough on the surface. Gently form a ball with the dough, and loosely cover it with plastic wrap.
5. When the oven is ready, carefully remove the pot. Uncover the bread and place it on a sheet of parchment paper. Lift the parchment paper with the dough on it, and place it into the pot. Cover the pot.
6. Bake for 30 minutes.
7. Remove the lid and bake for another 10 minutes.
8. Remove from the oven and cool the bread loaf on a wire cooling rack.
9. Slice and enjoy!

GAMING TIP

Trade one emerald to a village farmer and you could get a few loaves of bread!

23

STUFFED BROWN MUSHROOMS

Makes: 8–10 servings (24 mushrooms)

Mushrooms have tons of uses in *Minecraft and* in real life. If you're new to mushrooms, this is a great recipe to try them for the first time. The mushrooms are mild, and mostly act as a cup for loads of yummy spinach, cheese, and bread crumbs. For picky eaters, leave out the spinach and they'll still taste great.

INGREDIENTS:

- 24 cremini mushrooms
- 4 cups fresh, washed spinach
- 1 Tbsp. olive oil
- 1 Tbsp. minced garlic
- ½ cup Italian bread crumbs
- ½ cup shredded mozzarella cheese
- ¼ cup shredded Parmesan cheese

DIRECTIONS:

1. Preheat the oven to 400°F and line a baking sheet with foil. Set aside.
2. Remove the stems from the mushrooms. Wash them, pat them dry, and set the mushrooms, cavity-side up, on the foil-lined baking sheet. Chop the stems finely and set aside.
3. Cook the spinach in a pan until wilted, about 2 minutes. Remove the spinach from the pan, squeeze out all excess liquid, and chop fine.
4. Add 1 Tbsp. of olive oil and the minced garlic in a pan, and sauté for one minute.
5. Add the minced stems to the pan and sauté until soft, about 3 minutes.
6. Remove the pan from the heat and add the spinach, bread crumbs, and cheeses. Mix all of the ingredients together.
7. Using a small spoon, stuff the mushroom cavities with the mixture.
8. Bake for 20 minutes, or until the filling is golden on top and heated throughout.

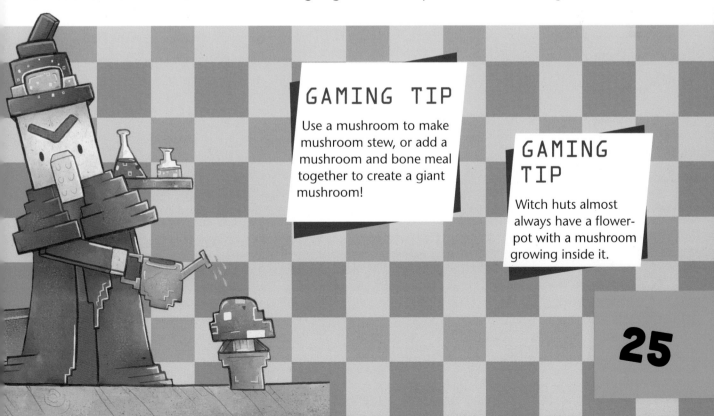

GAMING TIP

Use a mushroom to make mushroom stew, or add a mushroom and bone meal together to create a giant mushroom!

GAMING TIP

Witch huts almost always have a flower-pot with a mushroom growing inside it.

MAIN DISHES

BEETROOT SOUP

Makes: 6 servings

Beetroot soup may not be something you've tried before, but if you use this recipe, you'll discover that it's quite delicious! This recipe takes a classic, kid-friendly tomato soup recipe and adds in beets. The beets turn the soup bright pink and make the soup a little bit sweeter. Pair the soup with the Gold Block Sandwiches on page 30 for a warm and filling meal! (The soup's even tastier when you dunk the sandwich in it!)

28

INGREDIENTS:

- 2 (14.5-oz.) cans of diced tomatoes, drained
- 1 (15-oz.) can of whole beets, drained
- 1 (6-oz.) can of tomato paste
- 3 cups vegetable broth, *divided*
- 1 Tbsp. sugar
- ½ tsp dill
- ¼ tsp black pepper
- Salt and pepper

TOOLS:

- Blender
- Soup pot

DIRECTIONS:

1. Puree the tomatoes, beets, tomato paste, and ½ cup of vegetable broth in the blender.
2. Preheat a soup pot on the stove and place the tomato mixture and remaining broth in the pot.
3. Add the sugar, dill, and a dash of salt and pepper.
4. Bring the soup to a simmer, and then reduce heat to medium-low. Let cook for 30 minutes.

GAMING TIP

You can make beetroot soup with 6 beetroots and a bowl!

GAMING TIP

Beetroots are a key ingredient in red dye. If you want to turn a sheep's wool red, you'll need beetroot in your inventory.

GOLD BLOCK SANDWICHES

Makes: 1 serving

To many of us, cheese is a precious item that makes everything taste better. Treat it like gold with this delicious, game-inspired meal, served up in neat, little blocks. If any recipe can win over a picky eater in your family, it's this one. Serve on its own or with the Beetroot Soup on page 28.

INGREDIENTS:

- 1 Tbsp. butter
- 2 slices white bread
- 4 slices American or cheddar cheese

TOOLS:

- Butter knife
- Pan
- Spatula/food turner

DIRECTIONS:

1. Spread butter on both sides of each slice of bread.
2. Heat a pan on medium heat over the stove and cook the bread for 2 minutes on one side.
3. Carefully flip the bread over and top with the slices of cheese. Top with the slice of bread that doesn't have cheese on it, making sure the cooked sides are now in the middle of your sandwich.
4. Cook on one side for 2 minutes, then flip and cook on the other side for 2 minutes. The bread should be golden brown on every side!
5. Cut the sandwich into blocks before serving, stack them on a plate, and enjoy.

GAMING TIP

Blocks of gold can only be mined using an iron or diamond pickaxe. You need 9 gold ingots to craft the block yourself!

GOLD NUGGETS

Makes: 2–3 servings (8–12 nuggets)

Forget fast food: These healthy and yummy chicken nuggets are worth their weight in gold! Double the recipe to make dinner for the whole family. Get the most out of the nuggets' golden deliciousness by serving them with the Golden Carrot Dip on page 12.

INGREDIENTS:

- ½ cup flour
- Salt and pepper
- 1 egg
- 1 cup bread crumbs
- 1 tsp garlic powder
- 1 tsp onion powder
- 1 tsp oregano
- 2 Tbsp. olive oil
- 2 boneless, skinless chicken breasts

TOOLS:

- Two plates
- Whisk
- Small bowl
- Pan
- Sharp knife
- Spatula/food turner

GAMING TIP

Zombie pigmen may drop a gold nugget when killed. Want more? Kill them with a weapon enchanted with "looting." You may get up to 4 nuggets!

DIRECTIONS:

1. Prep a shallow plate with flour and a dash of salt and pepper. Set aside.
2. Whisk the egg with 1 tsp. of water in a bowl. Set aside.
3. Mix the bread crumbs, garlic and onion powder, oregano, a tsp. of salt and ½ tsp. of pepper in a shallow plate. Set aside.
4. Preheat a pan on the stove to medium heat. Once heated, add 2 Tbsp. olive oil.
5. Cut the chicken breasts into small, nugget shapes (about 1½ inches big each).
6. Dip the chicken into the flour mixture, coating it. Then, dip it in the whisked egg. Finally, dip it in the bread-crumb mixture, making sure the chicken is fully covered.
7. Carefully place the chicken nuggets into the pan and cook for 3 minutes on one side.
8. Flip the chicken nuggets to the other side and cook for approximately 3 minutes. The chicken is fully cooked when both sides are golden brown and there is no pink when you cut into the chicken. (Thick pieces may take a little longer.)
9. Serve plain or with your favorite dipping sauce!

**Wash your hands and work surface thoroughly after every time you come in contact with raw chicken or eggs.

HUNGER BAR DRUMSTICKS

Makes: 4–6 servings (10 drumsticks)

When you think of food in *Minecraft*, you most likely think of those delicious-looking drumsticks that make up your hunger bar. You can't live without 'em! Fill up your real-life hunger bar with these sweet, barbecue-flavored chicken drumsticks!

INGREDIENTS:

- 1 Tbsp. olive oil
- 1 cup ketchup
- ½ cup brown sugar
- 1 Tbsp. Worcestershire sauce
- 1 Tbsp. cider vinegar
- Salt and pepper
- 10 chicken drumsticks (one for each drumstick in your hunger bar!)

TOOLS:

- Medium bowl
- Large bowl
- Aluminum foil
- Baking sheet

DIRECTIONS:

1. Preheat the oven to 400°F and line a baking sheet with aluminum foil. Lightly oil the foil.
2. Mix the ketchup, brown sugar, Worcestershire sauce, and vinegar together until fully mixed. Season with a bit of salt and pepper.
3. Pour half of the sauce over the drumsticks in a large bowl and mix until they're fully covered.
4. Place the drumsticks on the foil-lined baking sheet.
5. Bake for one hour, brushing the drumsticks with additional sauce halfway through.
6. Remove the drumsticks from the oven and coat with the remaining sauce.

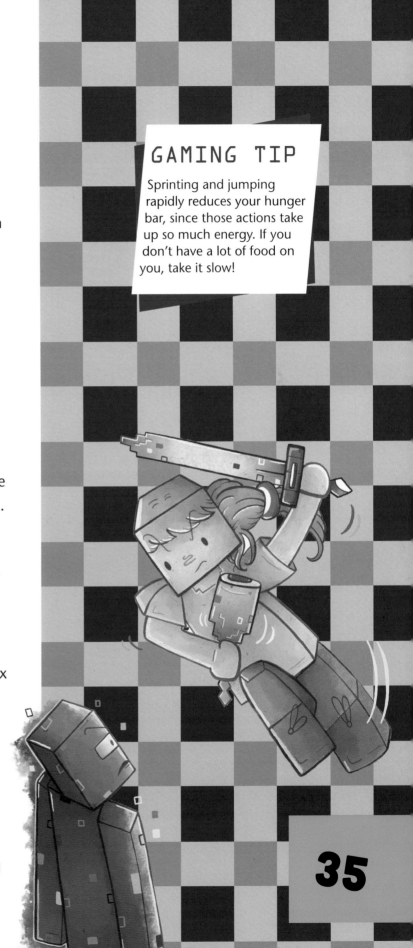

GAMING TIP

Sprinting and jumping rapidly reduces your hunger bar, since those actions take up so much energy. If you don't have a lot of food on you, take it slow!

SATISFYING COOKED PORK CHOPS

Makes: 2–3 servings (4 pork chops)

Cooked pork chops don't just relieve your hunger in-game. They make a fantastic and filling dinner for your whole family! Learn to make this recipe and pair it with the baked potato recipe on page 2 for a *Minecraft*-themed meal that will impress the grown-ups!

INGREDIENTS:

- 4 boneless pork chops, 1-inch thick
- 3 Tbsp. olive oil
- 2 tsp salt
- 1 tsp black pepper
- 1 tsp garlic powder
- 1 tsp thyme

TOOLS:

- Small bowl
- Baking sheet
- Meat thermometer (optional)

DIRECTIONS:

1. Preheat the oven to 400°F.
2. Rub each pork chop with olive oil.
3. Mix together the salt, pepper, garlic powder, and thyme in a small bowl, and sprinkle over all sides of the pork chops.
4. Place the pork chops on a baking sheet and bake for 15 minutes, or until a meat thermometer in a pork chop reaches 145°F.
5. Remove from the oven and rest for 3 minutes.
6. Serve with baked potatoes and your favorite veggie or salad!

GAMING TIP

Guess who drops pork chops? Pigs, when destroyed, leave them behind for you to collect.

37

ALMOST "RABBIT" STEW

Makes: 8 servings

Steve and Alex would both tell you that a rabbit stew is extremely hearty. It restores more hunger points than anything else in the game. In real life, the combination of meat, carrots, potatoes, mushrooms, and broth will keep you feeling full and warm. This stew uses chicken instead of rabbit, though you can throw in some rabbit-shaped pasta for a fun surprise!

INGREDIENTS:

- 1 Tbsp. olive oil
- 1½ lbs. of chicken meat, cut into 1-inch cubes
- ½ tsp salt
- ½ tsp pepper
- 2 potatoes, peeled and cubed
- 2 large carrots, cut into ½-inch pieces
- 1 medium onion, diced
- ½ cup sliced mushrooms
- 4 cups chicken broth
- 2 tsp dried basil
- 2 garlic cloves, minced
- 1 bay leaf
- 2 Tbsp. flour

TOOLS:

- Sharp knife
- Dutch oven or large pot

DIRECTIONS:

1. Heat a Dutch oven or large pot over the stove on medium-high heat. Place 1 Tbsp. of olive oil in the pot.
2. Cook the meat in the pot for a few minutes until it's browned on all sides. Season lightly with salt and pepper.
3. Add the potatoes, carrots, onion, mushrooms, broth, basil, garlic, bay leaf, and salt and pepper. Bring to a boil.
4. Once boiling, reduce the heat and let simmer, covered, for 20 minutes, or until the potatoes and carrots are tender.
5. Stir in the flour to help thicken the stew. Let simmer for 5 more minutes.
6. Remove the bay leaf, season with additional salt and pepper to taste, and serve!

COOKING TIP

Want to incorporate rabbits (and not rabbit meat)? Grab a box of mac and cheese with bunny-shaped noodles and add the noodles when the stew has 10 minutes left to simmer (about 5 minutes before step 5.)

my name is:
STEW

GAMING TIP

You can use a brown or a red mushroom (and any kind of cooked rabbit) to make rabbit stew in the game. When your avatar eats this stew, it makes a crunching sound instead of a slurping sound. Weird, right?

FISHERMAN'S SALMON

Makes: 4 servings (4 salmon fillets)

There are a variety of fish available in *Minecraft*, just like in real life. But a well-loved fish (both in-game and out) is salmon. It's healthy and so yummy that even people who don't normally like fish will enjoy it. Give this simple-yet-impressive recipe a try for dinner. Imagine you caught your salmon to survive the night!

INGREDIENTS:

- 1 Tbsp. olive oil
- 4 salmon fillets, around 6 oz. each
- 2 Tbsp. butter, melted
- 4 cloves of garlic, minced
- Juice of 2 small lemons
- Salt and pepper

TOOLS:

- Casserole dish or rimmed baking sheet
- Aluminum foil
- Small bowl

DIRECTIONS:

1. Preheat the oven to 375°F.
2. Line a casserole dish or rimmed baking sheet with aluminum foil, and lightly oil the foil.
3. Place the salmon fillets on the foil.
4. Mix the melted butter, garlic, and lemon juice in a small bowl and pour over the salmon fillets. Season with salt and pepper.
5. Move the edges of the foil up and around the salmon.
6. Cook in the oven for 15–20 minutes, or until the salmon flakes easily with a fork.

** Make sure to fully cook your fish both in-game and out before eating it!

GAMING TIP

Raw salmon only restores 2 hunger points and 0.2 saturation (and could poison you), while cooked salmon restores 6 points and 9.6 saturation!

MINECRAFT STEAK

Makes: 2 servings

Mmm . . . steak. Many people crave it, and will pay *a lot* to eat it a steak house. Now you can make like a chef at a fine restaurant and make your own incredible steak dinner! Serve your steak with other delicious sides (like the baked potatoes on page 2), and you can share it with even more people!

42

INGREDIENTS:

- 1 lb. sirloin steak, approximately 1 ½-inch thick
- 1 Tbsp. olive oil
- 1 tsp salt
- ¼ tsp pepper

TOOLS:

- Heavy pan

DIRECTIONS:

1. Let the steak sit until it's room temperature. (If it was in the fridge, this may take 30 minutes.)
2. Preheat a heavy pan on the stovetop at medium-high heat.
3. Rub all sides of the steak with olive oil.
4. Sprinkle salt and pepper all over the steak.
5. Place the steak in the pan and let cook for 4 minutes.
6. Turn the steak over and cook for another 4 minutes. (This will give you a medium steak. If you would like it more well-done, cook for an additional minute.)
7. Remove the steak from the pan and let it sit for 5 minutes.
8. Serve on its own, with steak sauce, or with some garlic-chive butter!

COOKING TIP

While the steak is cooking, whip up some delicious garlic-chive butter. It'll give your meal a steakhouse quality. It's easy. Just mix 2 Tbsp. butter (at room temperature), ½ Tbsp. minced chives, and 1 minced garlic clove together. When you're ready to serve your steak, put a spoonful of the butter on top.

GAMING TIP

Minecraft cows and mooshrooms drop raw beef when destroyed in the game. Cook that up in your furnace after a big battle and watch your hunger bar fill up!

LAPIS LAZULI PANCAKES

Makes: 4–6 servings (12 pancakes)

The beautiful lapis lazuli may not provide you with any hunger points in-game, but they do add a bright glimmer of color to an otherwise dark cave. Smelt a block of lapis lazuli and you'll have what you need to dye anything a vivid shade of blue. This recipe puts a Minecrafting spin on your favorite breakfast food and adds mega fun to your morning.

INGREDIENTS:

- 1 Tbsp. olive oil
- 1½ cups flour
- 2 Tbsp. sugar
- 2 tsp baking powder
- ¾ tsp salt
- 2 eggs
- 1 cup milk
- 1 tsp vanilla
- 3 Tbsp. melted butter
- Blue food coloring (for a dark blue color, use gel food coloring)
- ½ cup blueberries (can be fresh or frozen)
- Butter, syrup, and/or whipped cream (optional)

TOOLS:

- Griddle or large nonstick pan
- Large bowl
- Mixer
- ¼ cup measuring cup
- Spatula/food turner

DIRECTIONS:

1. Preheat a griddle to 350°F or a large nonstick pan to medium heat. Add a small amount of oil to the griddle or pan.
2. Whisk together the flour, sugar, baking powder, and salt in a large bowl. Set aside.
3. Beat the eggs, milk, and vanilla in a mixer until light and foamy (about 3 minutes). Add in the melted butter.
4. Pour the wet mixture into the dry mixture, and mix until smooth. Add a few drops of blue food coloring and mix until everything is the same color. Add more until you get the desired color.
5. Using a ¼ cup measuring cup, pour the batter onto the griddle in a "lapis lazuli" shape (kind of like a bean). Place 5–6 blueberries on top of the pancake. Cook for 2 minutes until bubbly and you can easily lift up the edges with a spatula. Flip and cook for an additional 2 minutes.
6. Continue until you've used up all of the batter.
7. Serve with whipped cream or butter and syrup!

GAMING TIP

Lapis lazuli can be used in a variety of ways in-game, including making other dye colors, dying objects (like beds, sheep, and dog collars), and even making blue fireworks!

BLAZE POWDER MAC AND CHEESE

Makes: 4 servings

How can you make macaroni and cheese even *better*? Add a dash of Blaze Powder. The fiery Blaze inspired this spicy mac and cheese recipe the whole family will love. If spicy food isn't your thing, substitute more white cheddar for the pepper jack and remove the chipotle chili powder altogether.

INGREDIENTS:

SAUCE:
- 2 Tbsp. butter
- 3½ Tbsp. flour
- 1½ cups whole milk
- 7 oz. white cheddar cheese, grated (about 1¾ cups)
- 1 oz. pepper jack cheese, grated (¼ cup)
- ½ tsp coarse salt
- ½ tsp chipotle chili powder
- ¼ tsp garlic powder
- ⅛ tsp black pepper

PASTA:
- 8 oz. macaroni pasta
- 1 oz. (¼ cup) white cheddar cheese, grated
- 1 oz. (¼ cup) pepper jack cheese, grated
- ½ tsp paprika
- 3 Tbsp. bread crumbs

TOOLS:
- Saucepan/small pot
- Whisk
- Wooden spoon
- A second pot (for cooking pasta)
- 8-inch casserole or baking dish

GAMING TIP

While Blaze Powder can be used to make a mundane potion or the potion of strength, it's also required fuel for the brewing stand itself. Make sure you have plenty of it on hand so you can craft the potions you need! Each Blaze Powder will last up to 20 brews.

DIRECTIONS:

1. To first make the sauce, melt butter in a medium saucepan over medium heat.
2. Once the butter has melted, whisk in the flour and continue to whisk and cook for 2 minutes.
3. Slowly add milk, whisking constantly.
4. Let sauce cook until it thickens, about 10 minutes, while stirring frequently.
5. Remove pan from heat and add the cheeses and seasonings listed in the "Sauce" section. Stir until everything is fully melted. Set aside.
6. Preheat the oven to 350°F.
7. Cook the macaroni according to the package, but remove 1 minute before the lowest cook time on the package directions. (It will continue cooking in the oven!) Rinse the pasta in cold water and let it drain.
8. Oil an 8-inch casserole dish and set aside.
9. Combine the cooked pasta with the sauce and mix until well coated. Pour the mac and cheese mixture into the casserole dish.
10. Cover the mac and cheese with the additional grated cheese, then the paprika, and then the bread crumbs.
11. Bake for 20 minutes or until the mac and cheese is bubbling and browned around the edges.

LILY PAD SALAD

Makes: 4 servings

To a Minecrafter, lily pads are very useful: they let you walk and build on water! Use spinach to represent lily pads and make a delicious salad with blueberries and blue dressing to represent water, and crunchy croutons to represent the blocks you can build with!

GAMING TIP

Have some water on a farm? Place a lily pad on it! You'll be able to get across it easily, but the water will still be able to get to the plants.

INGREDIENTS:

DRESSING:
- ¼ cup olive oil
- ¼ cup blueberries (fresh or frozen)
- 2 Tbsp. balsamic vinegar
- 1 Tbsp. honey
- ½ Tbsp. Dijon mustard

SALAD:
- 6 cups (5 oz.) spinach
- ½ cup fresh blueberries
- ½ cup crumbled feta
- ¼ cup sliced almonds
- ¼ cup croutons

TOOLS:
- Blender
- Large bowl
- Salad tongs

DIRECTIONS:

1. Make the dressing by placing all of the dressing ingredients into a blender and blending until smooth. Set aside.
2. Place all of the salad ingredients in a large bowl and add 2 Tbsp. dressing.
3. Using tongs, toss the salad until evenly mixed, and add more dressing to taste.
4. Separate the salad into four plates or bowls and serve.

DESSERTS

ALEX'S CHOCOLATE CHUNK COOKIES

Makes: 24 cookies

These cookies are bound to be your new favorite treat, and they use chocolate chunks to look even more like the pixelated cookies from the game. Cocoa beans and wheat are all you need to make them in *Minecraft*, but where's the fun in that? This recipe lets you enjoy mixing up lots of ingredients, using an electric mixer, and getting your hands as messy as you want. Alex would be so proud!

INGREDIENTS:

- 1 cup unsalted butter
- 1 cup brown sugar
- ½ cup sugar
- 2 eggs
- 1 tsp vanilla
- 2½ cups flour
- 1 tsp salt
- ¾ tsp baking soda
- 1 cup milk chocolate chunks
- 1 cup semisweet chocolate chunks

TOOLS:

- Mixer
- Medium bowl
- Plastic wrap
- Two cookie sheets
- Parchment paper
- Cookie scoop or spoon
- Wire cooling rack

COOKING TIP

Can't find chocolate chunks at the store? Get a chocolate bar and carefully dice it into ½-inch chunks!

DIRECTIONS:

1. Mix the butter in a mixer until it is light and creamy, then mix in both sugars.
2. One at a time, add in the eggs and the vanilla, mixing fully in between each addition.
3. Mix the flour, salt, and baking soda together in a separate bowl, and then slowly add into the wet mixture until everything is fully mixed.
4. Stir in the chocolate chunks.
5. Cover the top of the bowl of cookie dough with plastic wrap and refrigerate for one hour.
6. Fifteen minutes before the cookie dough comes out of the fridge, preheat the oven to 375°F. Cover the cookie sheets with parchment paper.
7. Using a cookie scoop or a spoon, drop round balls of cookie dough onto the cookie sheets, 2 inches apart from each other.
8. Bake for 8–9 minutes, or until the edges of the cookies are light brown.
9. Cool for 5 minutes and then transfer to a wire rack to finish cooling.

GAMING TIP

Cookies restore 2 hunger points, so they're great for players whose hunger bar is low. Be careful feeding them to unsuspecting *Minecraft* animals, though. If you feed one to a parrot in the game, they'll get poisoned and die!

ARCTIC BIOME SNOWBALL COOKIES

Makes: 36 cookies

You don't need to trek to an arctic biome or wait for cold weather to make these snowballs! Powdered sugar will give these cookies the realistic look of snow while making them even sweeter. Try to avoid throwing these snowballs anywhere but in your mouth!

INGREDIENTS:

- 1 cup unsalted butter, softened
- ¼ cup sugar
- 1 tsp vanilla
- A dash of salt
- 2 cups flour
- 2 cups pecans, finely chopped
- Powdered sugar

TOOLS:

- Two cookie sheets
- Parchment paper
- Large mixing bowl
- Medium bowl

DIRECTIONS:

1. Preheat the oven to 350°F and cover the cookie sheets with parchment paper.
2. Mix together the butter and sugar until smooth. Add the vanilla and salt and mix.
3. Slowly add in the flour and pecans until everything is well mixed.
4. Shape cookie dough into 1-inch balls. Place 1 inch apart onto the cookie sheet.
5. Bake 11–14 minutes or until very lightly browned.
6. Cool 5 minutes, then roll in some powdered sugar in a bowl.
7. Let cool completely and roll in powdered sugar once again.

GAMING TIP

Snow golems are your friends. They protect you by throwing snowballs at hostile mobs like zombies.

GINGERBREAD COOKIE CHESTS

Makes: 12 cookie chests

Coming across a chest while Minecrafting is so exciting. What treasures could be hiding inside? These cookie chests capture that same excitement, but with an edible twist. Roll, shape, and bake your way to a hollow, gingerbread box that can be filled with mini candies or sprinkles. Put your favorite treat inside each finished cookie chest and surprise your friends!

INGREDIENTS:

COOKIES:
- 3 cups flour
- 1 tsp baking soda
- ¼ tsp salt
- 2 tsp ginger
- 1 tsp cinnamon
- ¼ tsp nutmeg
- ¾ cup unsalted butter, room temperature
- ¾ cup brown sugar
- ½ cup molasses
- 1 egg
- 1 tsp vanilla
- 8 oz. mini M&Ms, sprinkles, or other small candies

ICING:
- 1½ cups powdered sugar
- 2 Tbsp. milk
- Black food coloring

TOOLS:
- Large bowl
- Mixer
- Plastic wrap
- Cutting board
- Rolling pin
- Two square or rectangle cookie cutters, one large and one small
- Two baking sheets
- Parchment paper
- Cooling rack
- Small bowl
- Two pastry bags or plastic ziplock bags

GAMING TIP
You can break a chest with anything, but an axe will get you inside it the fastest!

57

DIRECTIONS:

1. Mix the flour, baking soda, salt, ginger, cinnamon, and nutmeg together in a large bowl. Set aside.
2. Mix the butter and brown sugar in a mixer until light and fluffy.
3. Add molasses, egg, and vanilla to the butter mixture and mix well.
4. Slowly add the dry ingredients to the wet ingredients until everything is fully mixed.
5. Split the dough in half and form two balls. Flatten the balls into Frisbee shapes and wrap in plastic wrap.
6. Refrigerate for at least 1 hour.
7. Preheat the oven to 350°F.
8. Flour a cutting board or work surface and roll out the dough to ¼-inch thickness.
9. Using a square or rectangle cookie cutter, cut out shapes from the dough.
10. Using a smaller cookie cutter of the same shape, cut the center of ⅓ of the precut cookie shapes. Remove it, leaving a hollow square or rectangle outline. (Don't have a smaller cookie cutter? Using a butter knife, carefully cut out the center of ⅓ of the precut cookie shapes.)
11. Place cookie shapes on parchment paper-covered baking sheets.
12. Bake for 7 minutes, or until they begin to brown.
13. Remove the cookies from the oven and let cool on the pan for 5 minutes, then move to a cooling rack to cool completely.
14. While cooling, make the icing. Mix the powdered sugar and milk together until fully mixed and very sticky. Leave ¼ cup of the icing in the bowl and place the rest inside a plastic ziplock bag. When ready to ice, cut the very tip of one corner off, to make a piping bag.
15. Place one full cookie down and ice the bottom of one hollow cookie. Place on top of the full cookie.
16. Fill the cavity with some small candies or sprinkles. Pipe icing onto the top edges of the hollow cookie, and place another full cookie on top, so the hole is fully covered and it looks like a little chest.
17. Add a drop of black food coloring to the icing in the bowl and mix until it's gray. (Not gray enough? Add another drop of food coloring.)
18. Place the gray icing into another plastic ziplock bag and cut the tip off of the corner. Pipe a rectangle in the center of one side of the cookie, to look like the clasp of the chest.
19. Bite into or break a cookie to get to all of the goodies hidden in the "chest"!

SLIME BLOCKS

Makes: 24 blocks

These wiggly, slimy blocks are just like the bouncing green mobs in your favorite video game. You'll have a blast creating these jiggly gelatin squares complete with green maraschino cherry centers to represent the darker green center of the slime blocks. Dare your parents to eat them!

INGREDIENTS:

- 1 jar green maraschino cherries
- 2 packages (8 servings each) lime gelatin
- 2½ cups boiling water

TOOLS:

- 13x9-inch casserole dish
- Cooking spray
- Strainer
- Paper towels
- Large mixing bowl
- Knife

GAMING TIP

You may know that slime blocks are bouncy, but did you know that they can help you jump as high as 57½ blocks? Have you ever bounced that high?

DIRECTIONS:

1. Spray a 13x9-inch casserole dish with cooking spray.
2. Drain and rinse the cherries in a strainer. Remove the stems, and dry on paper towels.
3. In a large mixing bowl, carefully stir the gelatin and boiling water together until the gelatin has completely dissolved. Pour into the dish.
4. Carefully place 24 cherries in the gelatin-filled dish in a grid pattern.
5. Refrigerate for at least 3 hours, or until the gelatin is firm.
6. Dip the bottom of the dish in warm water for 15 seconds to help loosen the gelatin.
7. Cut the gelatin into 24 equal pieces, slicing each block around a cherry center.

59

CREEPER CRISPIES

Makes: 12 creepers

If you've played *Minecraft*, you've had a bad experience with a creeper. Normally you'd run away from creepers in fear, but Creeper Crispies will have the opposite effect on you! The green and gooey marshmallow treats are too delicious to be scary and they never, ever explode.

INGREDIENTS:

- 3 Tbsp. butter
- 4 cups marshmallows
- Green food coloring
- 6 cups crispy rice cereal
- Black decorating icing

TOOLS:

- 13x9-inch casserole dish
- Cooking spray
- Large microwave-safe bowl

DIRECTIONS:

1. Coat a 13x9-inch casserole dish with cooking spray.
2. In a microwave-safe bowl, heat butter and marshmallows in the microwave for 2 minutes. Stir, and microwave for 1 more minute. Stir until smooth.
3. Add a few drops of green food coloring and stir until everything is one color. If you'd like the green to be a bit darker, add a few more drops of coloring and stir again.
4. Add crispy rice cereal and stir until all cereal is well coated.
5. Spread the cereal out into the pan and let cool.
6. Cut into square shapes.
7. Using the black decorating icing, draw the creeper's face onto each square. (Use an image of a creeper as a guide.)

GAMING TIP

Did you know that creepers are afraid of cats? They'll run away from them faster than they'll run toward us! Tame an ocelot to protect yourself and your home.

DIRT BLOCK FUDGE

Makes: 16 squares

You'll find plenty of dirt blocks in the game of *Minecraft*, but none as good as these. This recipe is easy to follow and requires very few ingredients. All we did was leave out the dirt and replace it with oodles of tasty chocolate. Dig in!

INGREDIENTS:

- 3 cups milk chocolate chips
- 1 can (14 oz.) sweetened condensed milk
- 1 tsp vanilla extract

TOOLS:

- 8x8-inch square baking dish
- Wax paper
- Large microwave-safe bowl

DIRECTIONS:

1. Line an 8x8 baking dish with wax paper.
2. Place the chocolate chips and sweetened condensed milk into a large microwave-safe bowl, and microwave for 30 seconds at a time, stirring in between, until the chocolate chips are almost fully melted.
3. Add the vanilla extract and stir until everything is well mixed and smooth.
4. Spread the mixture into the baking dish.
5. Refrigerate for at least one hour, until the fudge is chilled and firm.
6. Lift the fudge out of the pan by the wax paper.
7. Cut into squares.

GAMING TIP

Dirt is the most common block in *Minecraft*. There are approximately 1,850 dirt blocks per chunk in most Overworld biomes! It can be found at any altitude and can be used for farming or building.

COOKING TIP

Turn the dirt blocks into Glowstone blocks by adding in ¼ cup Reese's Pieces right before spreading the mixture in the pan. (Prefer pure chocolate to peanut butter? Use yellow, orange, and brown M&Ms.)

63

ICE PLAINS BIOME BARK

Makes: 6–8 servings

The Ice Plains Biome is a rare biome with hardly any life. We're using white chocolate and fruit to re-create the look of this icy world and breaking it into pieces that resemble ice spikes! This makes a delicious mid-game treat. Make it before you start playing, and then take a break after 30 minutes to enjoy your chilled-and-ready creation.

INGREDIENTS:

- ½ cup blueberries
- ½ cup blackberries
- 16 oz. white chocolate chips
- Blue food coloring

TOOLS:

- 13x9-inch casserole dish
- Wax paper
- Microwave-safe bowl

DIRECTIONS:

1. Cover the 13x9 casserole dish with wax paper, letting some extra wax paper hang off the edges.
2. Rinse the blueberries and blackberries and pat dry.
3. Place the white chocolate chips in a microwave bowl and heat in a microwave for 30 seconds. Stir. Continue heating and stirring until the chocolate is melted and smooth.
4. Pour the melted white chocolate on top of the wax paper in the casserole dish. Slowly move the casserole dish around until the white chocolate is evenly covering the whole bottom.
5. Put a few drops of blue food coloring in various spots of the white chocolate. Drag a toothpick through the blue food coloring, swirling it around to make a cool design.
6. Place the blueberries and blackberries in the white chocolate, lightly pressing on them to make sure they'll stick.
7. Chill the mixture in the refrigerator for 30 minutes or more, until it is fully hardened.
8. Remove the mixture from the casserole dish by picking up the edges of the wax paper. Place on a counter.
9. Carefully break off pieces of the bark with your hands. It will break into different sizes and shapes, including ones similar to jagged ice spikes!

GAMING TIP

Although it's a difficult biome to survive in, Ice Plains offer some items that are almost impossible to find anywhere else. Keep your eyes open for white rabbits, polar bears, and igloos!

GOLDEN APPLES

Makes: 5 apples

A golden apple is extremely powerful, as it's the only food you can eat with a full hunger bar! While it may be difficult to find or make in-game, it's extremely easy to make IRL. You can use any type of apple you like for this classic caramel apple recipe, but I recommend Golden Delicious apples for the most "authentic" look.

INGREDIENTS:

- 5 apples
- 1 bag (14 oz.) of caramels, unwrapped
- 2 Tbsp. heavy cream

TOOLS:

- Baking sheet
- Wax paper
- 5 craft sticks
- Microwave-safe bowl

DIRECTIONS:

1. Prep a baking sheet with buttered wax paper.
2. Wash and thoroughly dry the apples.
3. Remove the stems from the apples and place craft sticks firmly into the center top of the apples.
4. Microwave caramels and heavy cream in a microwave-safe bowl for 2 minutes. Stir and let cool slightly.
5. Take an apple and dip into the caramel mixture, making sure to get the sides fully covered. Place on the buttered wax paper. Repeat.
6. Chill caramel apples in the refrigerator for 15 minutes or until ready to serve.

GAMING TIP

You can eat a golden apple (it will restore 4 points of hunger and 9.6 hunger saturation), but it can also be used to tame horses or to cure zombie villagers! To turn a zombie villager back into a normal one, use a golden apple and a potion of weakness.

GRASS BLOCK BROWNIES

Makes: 16 brownies

If there's one block that symbolizes one of the best computer games ever made, it's this one. These delicious brownies look just like a grass block, complete with chocolate chips for rocks and dirt clumps! Make grass grow on top of these sweet treats when you add a layer of bright-green frosting.

GAMING TIP

Grass just keeps on growing! If you have dirt blocks next to grass in an area with a light level of 9 or higher, the dirt blocks will slowly change into grass.

DIRECTIONS:

1. Preheat oven to 350°F.
2. Grease a 9-inch square baking pan.
3. Melt the semisweet chocolate chips and butter in a large saucepan over low heat. Stir until smooth and then remove from heat. Let cool for 2 minutes.
4. Stir the sugar into the chocolate butter mixture.
5. Add the eggs to the mixture one at a time, stirring between each egg.
6. Stir in the vanilla.
7. Mix the flour, salt, and baking soda in a small bowl. Add the dry mixture to the wet mixture and mix gently.
8. Stir in the milk chocolate chips.
9. Pour the brownie batter into the greased baking pan.
10. Bake for 45–50 minutes or until a toothpick inserted in the center comes out mostly clean (just a few crumbs).
11. Cool in the pan for 30 minutes.
12. While cooling, make the frosting: beat 1 cup of unsalted butter in a mixer until light and fluffy. Slowly add the powdered sugar, ½ cup at a time, mixing fully each time. Add the salt and vanilla, and mix for 2 minutes or until everything is light, fluffy, and the texture of a thick buttercream frosting. Add a few drops of green food coloring and mix until the color is even. Add more food coloring until you get the color of green you wish.
13. Place the frosting into a piping bag with a grass or star-shaped pastry tip on the bottom. Once the brownies are fully cooled, pipe the frosting onto the top of the brownies. (Don't have pastry tips? You can also frost the brownies with a butter knife or spatula!)
14. Slice the brownies into square shapes and enjoy!

INGREDIENTS:

BROWNIES:
- 1 cup semisweet chocolate chips
- ½ cup unsalted butter
- 1 cup sugar
- 3 eggs
- 1 tsp vanilla
- 1¼ cups flour
- ½ tsp salt
- ¼ tsp baking soda
- 1 cup milk chocolate chips

FROSTING:
- 1 cup unsalted butter, room temperature
- 2 cups powdered sugar
- ⅛ tsp salt
- 1 tsp vanilla
- Green food coloring

TOOLS:
- 9-inch square baking pan
- Large saucepan
- Small bowl
- Toothpick
- Mixer
- Piping bag or ziplock bag
- Grass or star-shaped pastry tip

HOME-CRAFTED PUMPKIN PIE

Makes: 1 9-inch pie

You don't need to wait until fall for this pumpkin pie! Make it any time of the year with canned pumpkin puree. The pie in *Minecraft* only requires a pumpkin, sugar, and an egg, but the pumpkin pie taste humans enjoy requires a touch of cinnamon, ginger, and nutmeg! Make like Alex and enjoy a little comfort food before heading out into battle.

INGREDIENTS:

- 9-inch piecrust (frozen, homemade, or prebaked)
- 1 (15-oz.) can pumpkin puree
- ½ cup sugar
- 1 tsp cinnamon
- ½ tsp ground ginger
- ½ tsp salt
- ¼ tsp nutmeg
- 2 eggs
- 1¼ cups evaporated milk
- Whipped cream (optional)

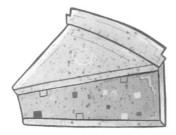

TOOLS:

- Pie plate
- Large bowl
- Butter knife
- Cooling rack

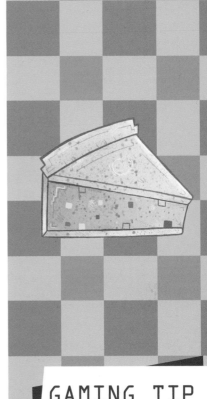

DIRECTIONS:

1. Preheat the oven to 425°F.
2. Place the piecrust in a pie plate.
3. Mix the pumpkin, sugar, and spices together in a bowl.
4. Add in the eggs, one at a time, mixing fully in between.
5. Slowly add in the evaporated milk until everything is mixed.
6. Pour the filling into the pie crust.
7. Carefully place the pie into the oven. Bake for 15 minutes.
8. Turn the oven temperature down to 350°F, and back for another 40 minutes, or until a knife inserted in the middle comes out clean. (The middle may still be a little wiggly.)
9. Remove from the oven and cool on a rack. (It may be 2 hours until it is completely cool!)
10. Serve with whipped cream.

GAMING TIP

While you shouldn't eat a whole pumpkin pie by yourself in real life, doing so in *Minecraft* is a-ok! It will restore 8 hunger points and 4.8 saturation.

MARSHMALLOW GHASTS

Makes: 1 serving (1 ghast)

Ghasts are a funny blend of cute and scary, but I can guarantee that you'll be safe from fireballs and creepy high-pitched sounds with this treat. These adorably creepy marshmallow ghasts have the perfect mix of sweet and salty, and assembling them from pretzels and marshmallows makes a great activity for friends and family to do together!

INGREDIENTS (PER GHAST):

- 2 oz. white chocolate chips
- 6 small pretzel sticks
- 1 large marshmallow
- Black decorating icing

TOOLS:

- Baking sheet
- Wax paper
- Microwave-safe bowl

DIRECTIONS:

1. Prep a baking sheet or other smooth surface with wax paper.
2. Place the white chocolate chips in a microwave bowl, and heat in a microwave for 30 seconds. Stir. Continue heating and stirring until the chocolate is melted and smooth.
3. Dip the pretzel sticks ⅔ of the way into the melted white chocolate. Let harden on the wax paper.
4. Insert pretzel stick "legs" into each marshmallow using the part that isn't covered in white chocolate, 3 in the front and 3 in the back.
5. Use the black decorating icing to draw eyes and a mouth on the marshmallows.

GAMING TIP

A bow and arrow is the best way to kill a ghast, but if you don't have one, try to hit a ghast fireball back at the ghast by knocking the fireball with your sword!

73

MUSHROOM CUPCAKES

Makes: 24 cupcakes

These mushroom cupcakes will be a hit at your next birthday party or game day! White chocolate chips and some food coloring transform vanilla cupcakes into your own Minecraft mushroom farm.

GAMING TIP

If you encounter a red cow called a "mooshroom" while playing, milk it with a bowl and you'll get mushroom stew!

DIRECTIONS:

1. Preheat the oven to 350°F.
2. Place cupcake liners in the cupcake tin.
3. Mix the flour, baking powder, and salt in a bowl. Set aside.
4. Beat the butter and sugar together in a mixer until light and fluffy.
5. Add eggs to the butter mixture, mixing fully between each egg. Mix in the vanilla.
6. Mix half of the dry ingredients into the wet mixture. Add half of the milk and mix. Continue with the rest of the dry ingredients and milk. Make sure everything is fully mixed.
7. Using an ice cream scoop or a large spoon, put one "scoop" of batter in each cupcake liner. They should be ¾ full.
8. Bake for 18–20 minutes, or until a toothpick inserted in the middle comes out clean.
9. Cool for 5 minutes in the tins, and then remove the cupcakes and cool completely on a wire rack.
10. Make the frosting: beat 3 cups of unsalted butter in a mixer until light and fluffy. Slowly add the powdered sugar, ½ cup at a time, mixing fully each time. Add the salt and vanilla, and mix for 2 minutes or until everything is light, fluffy, and the texture of a thick buttercream frosting. Add a few drops of red food coloring and mix, repeating until it's the color you would like.
11. Using an ice cream scoop, put a "scoop" of frosting on the top of a cupcake.
12. Carefully tip the cupcake over on wax paper and move the head of the cupcake around until the frosting forms a "dome" shape.
13. Decorate the top of your mushroom cupcake with 10-12 white chocolate chips by pushing them, tip down, into the frosting.
14. Repeat steps 12 and 13 with the rest of the cupcakes.

INGREDIENTS:

CAKE:
- 3 cups flour
- 2 tsp baking powder
- 1 tsp salt
- 1 cup unsalted butter, room temperature
- 2 cups sugar
- 3 eggs
- 2 tsp vanilla
- 1 cup milk

DECORATION:
- 1.5 cups unsalted butter, room temperature
- 3 cups powdered sugar
- ⅛ tsp salt
- 1 tsp vanilla
- Red gel food coloring
- White chocolate chips

TOOLS:
- Two cupcake tins
- 24 white cupcake liners
- Medium bowl
- Mixer
- Ice cream scoop or large spoon
- Toothpick
- Wire cooling rack
- Wax paper

75

"SPIDER EYE" CHERRIES

Makes: 30 cherries

Eating a spider eye? GROSS! It may fill a hunger bar slot, but it causes 2 hearts of damage, so you've got to be pretty desperate to eat one. These chocolate-covered cherries, with their ooey, gooey, cherry center, look just like spider eyeballs. The sweet centers get even more delicious if you let them sit for a few days, but no one could blame you for trying to sneak one earlier.

INGREDIENTS:

- ¼ cup maraschino cherry juice (from the jar)
- 1 (10-oz.) jar of maraschino cherries (with the stems)
- 4 cups powdered sugar
- 4 Tbsp. butter, softened
- 16 oz. white chocolate chips
- 10 oz. red candy melts

TOOLS:

- Small bowl
- Strainer
- Paper towels
- Two microwave-safe bowls
- Cookie sheet
- Wax paper
- Fork
- Airtight container

76

DIRECTIONS:

1. Pour the juice from the cherry jar out into a small bowl. Set aside.
2. Pour the cherries into a strainer and rinse them. Lay them out on a paper towel and gently pat them dry.
3. Combine the powdered sugar, ¼ cup of cherry juice, and butter together to form a fondant-style dough. Refrigerate for 20 minutes.
4. Roll the dough into small, 1-inch balls. Flatten the balls into a circle with your thumb.
5. Take a dough circle and wrap it around a cherry until it's covered up to the stem and forms a smooth ball.
6. Repeat with all cherries and then refrigerate for 20 minutes.
7. Place the white chocolate chips in a microwave bowl, and heat in a microwave for 30 seconds. Stir. Continue heating and stirring until the chocolate is melted and smooth.
8. Cover a cookie sheet with wax paper. Set aside.
9. Holding the stem, dip each cherry into the bowl of melted chocolate, fully covering it. Set on the wax paper-covered cookie sheet.
10. Place the red candy melts in a microwave bowl, and heat in a microwave for 30 seconds. Stir. Continue heating and stirring until the candy melts are melted and smooth.
11. Dip a fork into the bowl of melted red candy and drizzle it over the top of each cherry. Let candy coating run down the sides to resemble the veins of an eye.
12. Let candy coating sit until hardened, then transfer to an airtight container. Keep the container at room temperature for 3 days, or until the fondant centers turns gooey. Serve.

GAMING TIP

While these spider eyes are super edible, think twice before eating them in-game. They restore 2 hunger points and 3.2 saturation points, but apply a poison effect for 4 seconds!

POPPED CHORUS FRUIT BALLS

Makes: 10 popcorn balls

When chorus fruit gets smelted, it pops and becomes inedible. Just because you can't eat popped chorus fruit in the game doesn't mean you can't enjoy it in real life! Mix up this sweet and sticky, purple treat on an otherwise normal day and crank up the fun factor.

INGREDIENTS:

- 3 quarts (12 cups) popped popcorn
- ¼ cup butter
- 1 package (10½ oz.) mini marshmallows
- 1 box (3 oz.) grape gelatin
  (or combine 2 drops each, red and blue food coloring, until purple)

TOOLS:

- Rimmed baking sheet or casserole dish
- Wax paper
- Large microwave-safe bowl
- Nonstick cooking spray

DIRECTIONS:

1. Cover a rimmed baking sheet or large casserole dish with wax paper.
2. Put the popcorn on the baking sheet/dish and set aside.
3. Microwave butter and marshmallows in a large microwave-safe bowl for 90 seconds, or until the marshmallows get very large.
4. Add the gelatin powder (or food coloring) to the marshmallow mixture and stir.
5. Pour the marshmallow mixture over the popcorn.
6. Spray your hands with some nonstick cooking spray and mix the popcorn and the marshmallow mixture until all of the popcorn is coated.
7. Form the popcorn into small balls. Let cool completely on wax paper.

GAMING TIP

Popped chorus fruit is not edible, but you can use four of them to craft a purpur block. If you see a purpur block in the End, be careful. It could actually be the dangerous shulker hiding in its purple shell.

STEVE'S CREATIVE MODE CAKE

Makes: One 8-inch, two-layered cake

The cake is a fun and filling food item in *Minecraft* that players can share. Make your own real-life version of this yellow cake with vanilla frosting and cherries, perfect for any party or special occasion! While Steve has to farm to get his cake ingredients, you can just buy them at the grocery store.

INGREDIENTS:

CAKE:
- 2½ cups flour
- 2½ tsp baking powder
- ½ tsp salt
- ¾ cup unsalted butter, room temperature
- 1½ cups sugar
- 3 eggs, room temperature
- 1½ tsp vanilla
- 1¼ cups milk

DECORATION:
- 1½ cups unsalted butter, room temperature
- 3 cups powdered sugar
- ⅛ tsp salt
- 1 tsp vanilla
- 10 maraschino cherries

TOOLS:
- Two 8-inch square baking pans
- Medium bowl
- Mixer
- Toothpick
- Wire cooling rack
- Piping bag or ziplock bag
- Flat pastry tip
- Spatula or butter knife

DIRECTIONS:

1. Preheat the oven to 350°F.
2. Grease and flour 2 8-inch square baking pans.
3. Mix the flour, baking powder, and salt in a bowl. Set aside.
4. Beat the butter and sugar together in a mixer until light and fluffy.
5. Add eggs to the butter mixture, mixing fully between each egg. Mix in the vanilla.
6. Mix half of the dry ingredients into the wet mixture. Add half of the milk and mix. Continue with the rest of the dry ingredients and milk. Make sure everything is fully mixed.
7. Pour half of the cake mix in each pan.
8. Bake for 25–30 minutes, or until a toothpick inserted in the middle comes out clean.
9. Cool for 10 minutes in the pan, and then remove the cakes and cool completely on a wire rack.
10. Make the frosting: beat 1½ cups of unsalted butter in a mixer until light and fluffy. Slowly add the powdered sugar, ½ cup at a time, mixing fully each time. Add the salt and vanilla and mix for 2 minutes or until everything is light, fluffy, and the texture of a thick buttercream frosting.
11. Place the frosting into a piping bag with a flat pastry tip on the bottom.
12. Place one cake on a serving plate, and pipe frosting in a square shape in the middle of the top of the cake. Don't go all the way to the edge. Fill in the square with an even layer of frosting.
13. Place the second cake on top of the first frosted cake.
14. Pipe frosting on the top of the 2-layer cake. Carefully spread the frosting on top with a spatula or butter knife until it's smooth.
15. Pipe the square edges along the side of the cakes, using an image of the *Minecraft* cake as a guide. Fill them in.
16. Top the cake with cherries.

COOKING TIP

This makes a more realistic version of the *Minecraft* cake. Want one that looks just like the picture in-game? Use fondant. Place a sheet of white fondant over the top of the cake and cut squares along the side edges. Then cut squares out of red fondant and place those on top of the white fondant.

WHITE CHOCOLATE COBWEBS

Makes: Countless cobwebs

This technique is a super easy and fun way to make any chocolate cobweb shape you want. Cobwebs may slow you down in the game, but they will make you jump for joy when you get to shape them out of pure chocolate! After you make White Chocolate Cobwebs and get them looking like the ones in the game, experiment with other types of chocolate (milk chocolate and dark chocolate make amazing webs, too) and different web designs.

GAMING TIP

Almost everything (including mobs, players, and items) move a little bit more slooooowly when going through a cobweb. The only exceptions are spiders and cave spiders, of course!

INGREDIENTS:

• One bag of white chocolate chips

TOOLS:

• Baking sheet
• Wax paper
• Microwave-safe bowl
• Piping bag or ziplock bag

DIRECTIONS:

1. Prep a baking sheet or other smooth surface with wax paper.

2. Place the white chocolate chips in a micro-wave bowl, and heat in a microwave for 30 seconds. Stir. Continue heating and stirring until the chocolate is melted and smooth.

3. Carefully pour the melted chocolate into a piping bag or ziplock bag with the corner tip cut off.

4. Carefully cut the tip of one of the bag corners.

5. Use the chocolate to draw an image of a cobweb directly onto the wax paper. Start with a cross, and then put an "X" directly over it. Then, draw a small circle around the center and a slightly larger one around the middle of the cobweb. (See the cobweb illustrations on this page for reference.)

6. Continue to make cobwebs until you use up all the chocolate!

7. Let cool until fully hardened. This can be done at room temperature, or in the fridge if you're in a hurry.

COOKING TIP

Want your cobweb to look exactly like the ones from Minecraft? Print off an image of a cobweb and place the image underneath the wax paper. Then just trace the image with your drizzled stream of chocolate!

DIAMOND CANDY

Makes: One string of diamond candy

Grow your own edible, blue diamonds in the kitchen—no actual mining necessary! This is a crafty but simple science experiment that every kid will enjoy. Be patient, though: you'll get the best results if you leave it overnight. Get creative and create candy gems in different colors: try green for emeralds and purple for End crystals.

INGREDIENTS:

- ½ cup water
- 1 cup sugar
- 2–3 drops blue food coloring

TOOLS:

- 12-oz. mason jar
- Cotton thread
- Tape
- Pencil
- Small saucepan
- Plastic wrap

GAMING TIP

Diamonds are one of the rarest materials in *Minecraft* and can be used to make the most powerful tools and armor. If you end up with too many diamonds (if there's such a thing), you can unlock an achievement called "Diamonds to You" by throwing a diamond at another player!

DIRECTIONS:

1. Clean and dry a 12-oz. mason jar.
2. Cut a thick cotton thread a few inches larger than the height of the jar.
3. Wet the thread with water and roll in a little bit of sugar.
4. Tape the end of the thread to a pencil and balance the pencil over the top of the jar. Roll the pencil to wind up the thread until there's a little bit of space between the end of the thread and the bottom of the jar.
5. Place the water in a small saucepan on a stove and bring the water to a boil. Slowly add in the sugar, stirring until it dissolves.
6. Remove the pan from the heat and add one drop of blue food coloring. Mix until everything is the same color.
7. Cool for 10 minutes, and then pour the sugar syrup into the jar.
8. Cover the jar loosely with plastic wrap and keep in a cool place. Check up on it daily until the diamond candy is as large as you would like it! (You'll see some changes after a few hours, but it could take a week or more for it to get as large as you'd like.)
9. Remove the diamond candy from the jar, dry it, and eat it!

PORTAL COOKIES

Makes: About 20 cookies

These Portal Cookies look like they'll lead you straight into another world, but instead you'll pop them straight into your mouth for a chewy plus crunchy flavor adventure! They take a little extra time and effort to make, but the reward of having an edible portal will make it worth it.

INGREDIENTS:

- 3 cups flour (plus additional for dusting)
- ¾ tsp baking powder
- ¼ tsp salt
- 1 cup (2 sticks) unsalted butter, at room temperature
- 1 cup sugar
- 2 eggs
- 1 tsp vanilla extract
- 5 orange hard candies, 5 yellow hard candies, 5 red hard candies (Jolly Ranchers work best)

TOOLS:

- Large bowl
- Mixer
- Plastic wrap
- Plastic ziplock bag
- Kitchen towel
- Wooden mallet or rolling pin
- 1 large square cookie cutter and 1 small square cookie cutter
- Cookie sheet
- Parchment paper

DIRECTIONS:

1. In a large bowl, mix the flour, baking powder, and salt together. Set aside.
2. In a mixer, beat the butter and sugar together until fully mixed and light and fluffy.
3. Add eggs and vanilla to the butter and sugar mixture and mix on low until combined.
4. Slowly add the flour mixture until everything is combined.
5. Scrape the sides of the mixer to make sure you didn't miss anything, and mix one more time.
6. Remove the dough and roll into a log. Cover with plastic wrap and refrigerate for at least 30 minutes.
7. While the dough is chilling, place the hard candies in a plastic ziplock bag, wrap the bag in a kitchen towel, and carefully hit the candies with a wooden mallet or rolling pin until they are in small pieces. Set aside.
8. When ready to bake, preheat the oven to 350°F and line a cookie sheet with parchment paper.
9. Prepare your work surface (a large cutting board or counter) by dusting with flour and roll out your cookie dough to ¼-inch thick.
10. Cut large squares out, and then cut 4 small squares out of each large square, to make it look like a trapdoor.
11. Place the cutout cookies onto the parchment paper-lined cookie sheet and bake for 8 minutes.
12. Using an oven mitt, carefully remove the cookie sheet from the oven and place on the stove.
13. Take the small hard candy pieces and put them in each of the 4 squares inside each cookie, so they're touching the parchment paper. (Mix the colors together so it looks like lava!)
14. Bake for another 3 minutes or until the cookies start to brown on the edges and the candy has melted.
15. Cool on the cookie sheet for 5 minutes and then move to a wire rack until completely cooled.

DRINKS

BONE MEAL COCOA MIX

Makes: 24 servings

This recipe looks like bone meal, but thankfully doesn't use bones as an ingredient. The vitamins in this white cocoa powder are great for your bones, though! This recipe makes enough cocoa powder for 24 servings, so save it in an airtight container or invite a bunch of friends over for a cocoa-and-*Minecraft* night.

INGREDIENTS:

- 3 cups dry milk powder
- 2 cups powdered sugar
- 1½ cups unsweetened cocoa powder
- 1½ cups white chocolate chips
- 20 chocolate sandwich cookies
- ¼ tsp salt
- 1 cup milk (per serving)
- Whipped cream (optional)
- Additional chocolate sandwich cookies (optional)

TOOLS:

- Large bowl
- Blender or food processor
- Airtight container

DIRECTIONS:

1. Mix all ingredients together in a large bowl.
2. Using a blender or food processor, pulse the ingredients until it forms a fine powder. (If your blender/food processor is not large enough to hold everything, work in 2 or 3 batches.)
3. Store the mix in an airtight container. The powder will last for up to 3 months.
4. To turn this into hot cocoa, mix ⅓ cup of the powder mix with 1 cup of hot milk in a mug. Top with whipped cream and some additional crushed cookies if desired!

GAMING TIP

Bone meal can be used as a fertilizer for farming or as a white dye. Try mixing it with other dyes to make lighter colors!

LIQUID LAVA SODA

Makes: One 12-ounce drink

Finally, a drinkable lava that won't do you any physical harm! This recipe makes one fiery-colored, 12-ounce drink. If you want to serve it in a way that's true to the game, pour the whole batch into a small beach bucket and serve it from there!

INGREDIENTS:

- 4 oz. orange juice
- 7 oz. lemon-lime soda
- 1 oz. grenadine

TOOLS:

- Cup
- Spoon or straw

DIRECTIONS:

1. Pour the orange juice and lemon-lime soda into a cup.
2. Slowly add the grenadine and watch it fall to the bottom.
3. Keep the drink layered, or stir it with a spoon or straw to mix the colors together.

GAMING TIP

Need to stop a flow of lava from destroying you or your possessions? Put up a ladder or a sign! Those will prevent the lave from flowing past.

POTION OF FIRE RESISTANCE MILKSHAKE

Makes: One milkshake

While I can't guarantee this version of the potion will help you resist ACTUAL fire, this caramel milkshake could help cool your mouth after you eat something spicy! Milk helps dissolve the chemical compound found in spicy food that makes your tongue burn. How neat is that?

INGREDIENTS:

- 2 cups vanilla ice cream
- 1 cup milk
- ⅓ cup caramel syrup

TOOLS:

- Blender
- Glass

DIRECTIONS:

1. Place all of the ingredients into a blender.
2. Blend until smooth.
3. Pour into a glass.

GAMING TIP

Potions of fire resistance give immunity to all kinds of heat-related damage (blaze attacks, ghast fireballs, and lava, for example). You can brew it by adding nether wart and magma cream to a water bottle. Use it to fight blazes!

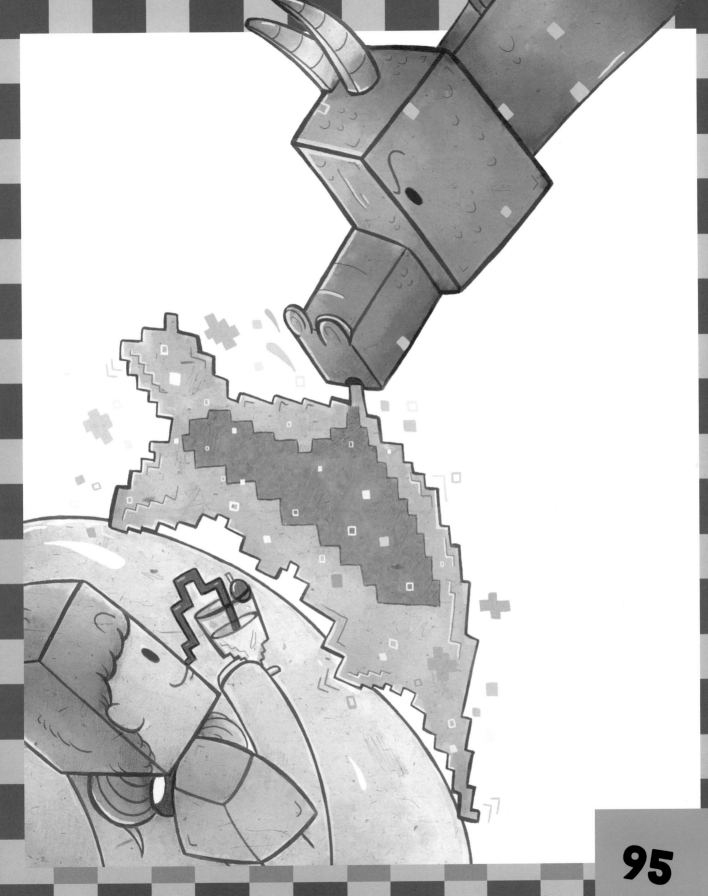

POTION OF HEALING MELON COOLER

Makes: 6 servings

A Potion of Healing is made from a sparkly fruit in *Minecraft* called glistering melon. Glistering melon may be make-believe, but watermelon is a worthy substitute! This recipe will make enough refreshing melon "potion" for a table-full of tired, young warriors.

INGREDIENTS:

- 1 watermelon
- 4 cups lemon-lime soda
- Whipped cream
- Red sprinkles

TOOLS:

- Spoon
- Blender
- Fine mesh strainer
- 4 glasses

DIRECTIONS:

1. Slice the watermelon in half and scoop out the insides.
2. Blend the watermelon insides in a blender.
3. Using a fine mesh strainer, strain the juice from the blended watermelon pulp.
4. Mix the juice with the lemon-lime soda.
5. Pour into glasses and add whipped cream and sprinkles.

GAMING TIP

A Potion of Healing restores 4 health. You can make it by adding nether wart and glistering melon to a water bottle.

POTION OF NIGHT VISION SMOOTHIE

Makes: One smoothie

When night falls in *Minecraft*, things get a lot more dangerous for Steve and Alex. Potion of Night Vision helps by allowing players to see approaching zombies and creepers before they strike. Want to improve your night vision? Add Vitamin A to your diet. This Potion of Night Vision drink is full of Vitamin-A foods like carrots and spinach, but all the flavor comes from delicious fruits and a dose of honey! Turn the lights out after you drink this smoothie and see how much night vision power you have.

INGREDIENTS:

- 1 carrot, diced (or 5–6 baby carrots)
- 1 cup spinach, loosely packed
- ¾ cup frozen blueberries
- ½ cup frozen strawberries (approximately 4–5 whole berries)
- ⅔ cup apple juice
- 1 Tbsp. honey

TOOLS:

- Blender
- Glass

DIRECTIONS:

1. Place all of the ingredients into a blender.
2. Blend until smooth.
3. Pour into a glass.

GAMING TIP

A Potion of Night Vision will let you see in the dark (it will visually brighten everything to a light level of 15) and let you see better underwater! You can make it by adding nether wart and a golden carrot to a water bottle.

POTION OF STRENGTH POWER DRINK

Makes: One power drink

Just like the potion in the game, this "potion" drink is packed with protein and vitamins to make you as strong as you can be. Plus, it tastes just like a PB&J sandwich! Make one for an easy breakfast to take on the go. Power up with this tasty drink and you'll have energy to spare.

INGREDIENTS:

- 1 banana
- 1 cup frozen mixed berries
- 2 Tbsp. peanut butter (or other nut butter of your choice)
- ½ cup milk
- 1 tsp honey

TOOLS:

- Blender
- Glass

DIRECTIONS:

1. Place all of the ingredients into a blender.
2. Blend until smooth.
3. Pour into a glass.

GAMING TIP

A Potion of Strength will increase your attack damage by 3! You can make it by adding nether wart and blaze powder to a water bottle.

101

POTION OF LEAPING SHERBET FLOAT

Makes: 12 servings

This bright green, fizzy drink definitely looks and feels like a potion! This is the perfect drink for a *Minecraft*-themed party. Share with friends or family and practice leaping like you've never leaped before. Imagine you are in the Nether bounding over burning-hot lava pits. Add a festive feel to any regular day with this celebratory sherbet float.

INGREDIENTS:

- 2 liters lemon-lime soda
- 1 quart lime sherbet
- Green Pop Rocks

TOOLS:

- Punch bowl or separate glasses
- Ice cream scoop

GAMING TIP

A Potion of Leaping will let you jump higher and reduce fall damage. You can make it by adding nether wart and a rabbit's foot to a water bottle. Add some glowstone dust, and the potion will be stronger, but will only last half the time.

DIRECTIONS:

1. Pour the lemon-lime soda into a punch bowl or in separate glasses.
2. Using an ice cream scoop, scoop all of the sherbet into the punch bowl, or one scoop per glass.
3. Sprinkle green Pop Rocks on the top of the potion for additional "jumping" action.

REDSTONE DUST SHAKE

Makes: 1 shake

Redstone is what makes any machine work when you're Minecrafting. This colorful drink pays tribute to the dust that can set off a TNT block, open an iron door, or trap a creeper. Use strawberry-flavored powder as redstone, add some frozen berries, and create an other-worldly drink! It'll be sure to power you through any day.

INGREDIENTS:

- 2 Tbsp. "Nesquik" strawberry-flavored powder
- 1 cup milk
- 2 cups vanilla ice cream
- 1 cup frozen strawberries

COOKING TIP

Want the drink's color to be darker red like the in-game powder? Add a couple drops of red food coloring before blending.

TOOLS:

- Blender
- Glass

DIRECTIONS:

1. Mix the strawberry-flavored powder into the milk.
2. Place the milk, ice cream, and frozen strawberries into a blender.
3. Blend until smooth.
4. Pour into a glass.

GAMING TIP

Plan on making a complex machine with Redstone? Plan it out in advance by making it in Creative Mode. Take notes on how many blocks you use and where everything goes. Then you can re-create it more quickly and easily in Survival Mode!

GLOSSARY

baking sheet: A rectangular metal tray that fits in the oven.

blend: To break up pieces into a powder or liquid in a blender. Blending may result in multiple ingredients being mixed together.

blender: An electric tool with spinning blades that can mix, chop, and liquify ingredients. Often used for smoothies and milkshakes.

candy melts: An easy-to-melt product that is similar to white chocolate. It's available in a variety of colors and flavors at craft and baking supply stores.

chop: To cut into smaller pieces with a knife.

cooling rack: A wire rack that warm food can sit on until it cools. (The holes in the rack allow airflow to help cool the food.)

dash: A small amount of an ingredient. Examples: A quick shake of a salt shaker, or a small pinch of a spice.

dice: Cut into small cubes.

dry ingredients: Any item that is dry. Often includes items found in your pantry or cabinet.

fondant: A thick, clay-like paste made of sugar and water. Often rolled out into sheets and used to decorate cakes.

grenadine: A red syrup, often cherry-flavored. Found in the drink mixers section in the grocery store, it's a common ingredient in Shirley Temples.

mince: To cut up into very small pieces.

mix: To combine two or more ingredients together.

mixer: A tool that allows you to mix ingredients more easily. Common versions are stand mixers and hand mixers (or eggbeaters). If you don't have a mixer, you can mix with your hand using a whisk or wooden spoon.

oven rack: The metal racks in an oven. These can be carefully moved to different levels in the oven. For most recipes, place your food on a rack in the middle of the oven.

pastry tip: A metal tip with a shaped hole through it used with frosting and cream. Pastry tips are placed in the bottom in a piping bag.

peeler: A tool that shaves the top layer of items. Often used for potatoes, fruits, and vegetables.

piping bag: A large cone-shaped bag to hold frosting and give you better control over decorating with it. If you do not have a piping bag, you can cut the corner off of a plastic ziplock bag and fill that.

powdered sugar: A very fine grain of sugar used in pastries. Also known as "confectioner's sugar."

preheat: To turn the oven on and let it heat until it gets to the correct temperature.

pulse: To blend with multiple short blasts instead of one steady stream.

quarter: To cut into four pieces. Cut in half one way, and then turn and cut it in half the other way.

stir: To mix ingredients together with a spoon or other utensil.

strainer: A bowl with very small holes or mesh to separate liquid from solids. Great for rinsing food in the sink.

Tbsp: Tablespoon

tsp: Teaspoon

wet ingredients: Any ingredient that is wet. Often includes items found in the refrigerator.

whisk: A tool with wire or flexible loops used to mix ingredients or beat eggs.

Acknowledgments

You're more successful when building as a team in *Minecraft*, and the same could be said about this book. Thank you to the following people for assisting with the creation of this book.

Editor:
Aimee Chase

Food Photography:
Allan Penn
Jen Glovsky

Illustrations:
Grace Sandford

Expert Guidance:
Aidan and Colin Telford

Recipe Testers:
Richelle Bixler
Yesenia Cisneros
Evie, Pete, and Tori Courtney
Daniel Helmick
Kayce Marzolf
Liz Smith

And thank you to Vince Miller and Andreas Theoharis for letting me repurpose some classic family recipes!

INDEX

CONVERSION CHARTS

METRIC AND IMPERIAL CONVERSIONS
(THESE CONVERSIONS ARE ROUNDED FOR CONVENIENCE)

Ingredient	Cups/Tablespoons/ Teaspoons	Ounces	Grams/Milliliters
Butter	1 cup/ 16 tablespoons/ 2 sticks	8 ounces	230 grams
Cheese, shredded	1 cup	4 ounces	110 grams
Cream cheese	1 tablespoon	0.5 ounce	14.5 grams
Cornstarch	1 tablespoon	0.3 ounce	8 grams
Flour, all-purpose	1 cup/1 tablespoon	4.5 ounces/0.3 ounce	125 grams/8 grams
Flour, whole wheat	1 cup	4 ounces	120 grams
Fruit, dried	1 cup	4 ounces	120 grams
Fruits or veggies, chopped	1 cup	5 to 7 ounces	145 to 200 grams
Fruits or veggies, pureed	1 cup	8.5 ounces	245 grams
Honey, maple syrup, or corn syrup	1 tablespoon	0.75 ounce	20 grams
Liquids: cream, milk, water, or juice	1 cup	8 fluid ounces	240 milliliters
Oats	1 cup	5.5 ounces	150 grams
Salt	1 teaspoon	0.2 ounce	6 grams
Spices: cinnamon, cloves, ginger, or nutmeg (ground)	1 teaspoon	0.2 ounce	5 milliliters
Sugar, brown, firmly packed	1 cup	7 ounces	200 grams
Sugar, white	1 cup/1 tablespoon	7 ounces/0.5 ounce	200 grams/12.5 grams
Vanilla extract	1 teaspoon	0.2 ounce	4 grams

OVEN TEMPERATURES

Fahrenheit	Celsius	Gas Mark
225°	110°	¼
250°	120°	½
275°	140°	1
300°	150°	2
325°	160°	3
350°	180°	4
375°	190°	5
400°	200°	6
425°	220°	7
450°	230°	8